Photo © Richard Day/Daybreak Imagery; ruby-throated male hummingbird

page one

# Ruby-throated Hummingbirds
## (Archilochus colubris)

Named for their metallic red gorgets, these birds are small in size (about 3-3½ inches long) with glimmering emerald coloring around their backs and wings. The female has a white patch under her throat, a longer beak, shorter tail and will be larger in size than the male. Ruby-throated hummingbirds don't pair up; the female builds the nest and takes care of her young by herself, while the male only participates in fertilization. The sexes even migrate separately, with the males leaving their seasonal areas weeks before the females.

Of the fifteen species of hummingbird that are spotted in North America, this is the only one that nests east of the Mississippi River. Ruby-throated hummers migrate across the Gulf of Mexico twice a year, from late February to early March, they travel up into eastern Canada and the United States, by November most will have spread into Mexico and Central America for the winter.

Their nests can be found in hardwood and conifer forests, meadows, wetlands, along hillsides and in gardens, parks and urban areas. These hummingbirds consume nectar from flowering plants, and are particularly fond of honeysuckle, trumpet vine and mint. Both the females and males are quite territorial and aggressively defend their feeding zones.

Photo © Richard Day/Daybreak Imagery, ruby-throated male hummingbird

Photo © Richard Day/Daybreak Imagery, ruby-throated male hummingbird

Photo © Todd Fink/Daybreak Imagery, ruby-throated hummingbird

page three

# Ruby-throated Hummingbirds (Archilochus colubris)

*Ruby-throated  
Nest Series*

Photos © Richard Day/Daybreak Imagery,
ruby-throated hummingbirds

# Rufous Hummingbirds
## (Selasphorus rufus)

Known for the rufous or red coloring on its head and body, these birds are medium sized, ranging between 3½ and 4 inches in length. The females are slightly larger than the males, with green backs and rufous on their flanks and tail feathers.

The rufous flies farther north than any other hummingbird, nesting from southern Alaska and the west coast of British Columbia, down into Washington, Idaho, Montana and Oregon. Because they winter in Mexico and Central America, they have the longest flight, across the Continental Divide, through mountainous regions that peak around 13,000 feet. With their ability to fly at such high altitudes and over long distances, the rufous have an incredible endurance for cold temperatures, making this species the hardiest of all hummingbirds.

They settle in mixed forests, meadows, chaparral and along the coast to above the timberline, feeding on high nectar-producing flowers. Favorite flowers include: Indian paintbrush, fireweed, salmonberry, red columbine, honeysuckle, bee plant, manzanita and agave. The rufous hummingbird is considered to be the most aggressive species, perching high above its food sources and violently attacking anything that violates its territory.

Photo © Frank Cleland/Gnass Photo Images, female rufous hummingbird

Photo © Steve Aulston, female rufous hummingbird

Photo © Hugh P. Smith, Jr., male rufous hummingbird

page seven

# Broad-tailed Hummingbirds
## (Selasphorus platycercus)

Similar to both the ruby-throated and calliope hummingbird, the broad-tailed hummer is larger in size, measuring from 4-4½ inches in length with a metallic green back and head, ruby throat and green coloring on its sides. The female appears smaller and has a white chin and throat.

Broad-tailed hummingbirds breed in the mountains of the southwest (western Texas, Nevada, Arizona, Colorado, Utah and Wyoming) and winter in Mexico. Mature male broad-tails are the only hummingbirds that produce a continuous sharp chirp or staccato whistle during normal flight. The sound is produced by wind that moves through a slot formed by tapered tips on its ninth and tenth primary wing feathers. It is speculated that the broad-tailed uses this whistle as a warning to other birds that enter its territory.

The broad-tailed hummer lives in the open woods and meadows of mountainous areas, frequently nesting in aspens, pinyons, oak stands and juniper trees. They feed on nectar-rich flowers and small insects, and follow the mountain flowers as they bloom. The most attractive blossoms to the broad-tailed hummingbird are yucca, agave, columbine, mint and bouvardia.

Photo © Steve Aulston, broad-tailed male hummingbird

page eight

Photo © Steve Aulston, broad-tailed hummingbird

# Broad-tailed Hummingbirds (Selasphorus platycercus)

Photo © Frank Cleland/Gnass Photo Images, broad-tailed, female hummingbird

page ten

# Allen's Hummingbirds
## (Selasphorus sasin)

Allen's hummingbird is one of the smallest species found in North America, measuring less than 4 inches in length. It is similar to the rufous, except for its green head and back. The females have green or bronze-green backs with spotted throats and tend to be a bit smaller than the males.

These birds establish permanent breeding colonies along the California coast and the southernmost parts of Arizona. They are one of the few species that winter in the United States, although they also migrate into Mexico and along the Baja peninsula. Damp ravines and canyons are their typical nesting spots, especially among low brush (blackberry is the most common).

Droughts during the 1980s and 1990s were estimated to have reduced the population of Allen's hummingbirds by as much as 90%. Private birdfeeders spread across their migration route were thought to have saved the species from complete extinction.

Photo © Steve Aulston, Allen's, male hummingbird

# *Allen's Hummingbirds* (Selasphorus sasin)

Photo © Hugh P. Smith, Jr., Allen's female hummingbird

page twelve

Photo © Hugh P. Smith, Jr., Allen's hummingbird and babies

Photo © Hugh P. Smith, Jr., baby Allen's hummingbirds

page thirteen

# Calliope Hummingbirds
## (Stellula calliope)

Measuring from 2.8-3.5 inches long, the calliope is the smallest hummingbird in North America. Its appearance is similar to that of the broad-tailed hummer, but smaller. Females are larger in size and have green striping down their throats; male calliopes have magenta striping.

They migrate from the western states into British Columbia and Saskatchewan, and winter in central and western Mexico. Calliopes breed in the high mountains, building their nests over creeks or in brush along riverbeds. One of the ways to identify a calliope hummingbird is to observe how low it flies. They tend to zoom in about the first four or five feet above the ground. They also tend to nest at this level, making it easier for them to chase down and catch small insects for food.

Calliope hummingbirds are quite territorial and very protective; they are often seen chasing away birds twice their size. Because they live so close to the ground, their nests are protected by foliage and nestled among pine cones or covered with lichens. These birds can be attracted to gardens by placing feeders about a foot above the ground in areas that contain bushes or some sort of cover.

Photo © Frank Cleland/ Ginass Photo Images, calliope female hummingbird

Photo © Frank Cleland/ Gnass Photo Images, calliope female hummingbird

Photo © Hugh P. Smith, calliope female hummingbird

Photo © Steve Aulston, calliope female hummingbird

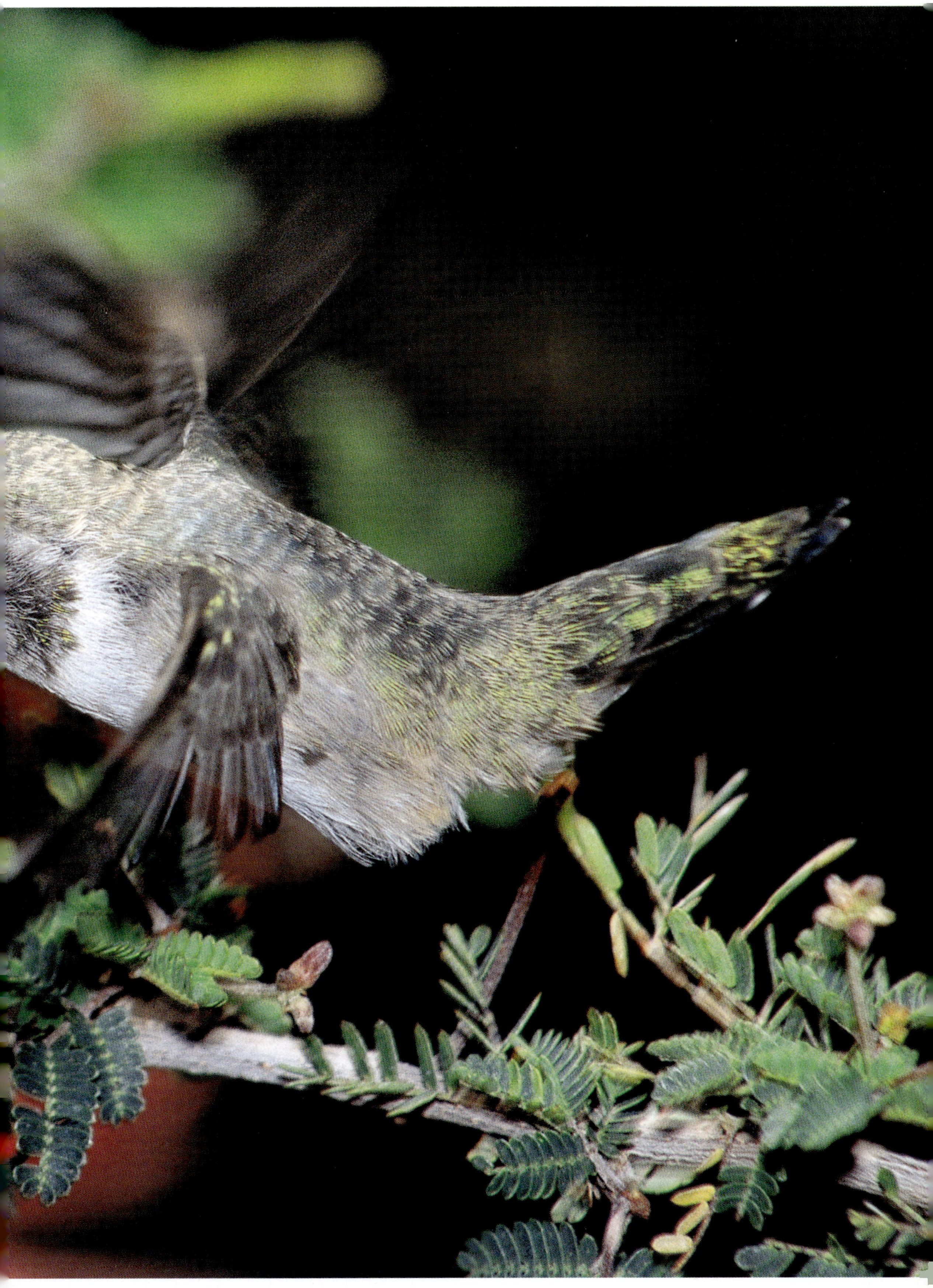

# Magnificent Hummingbirds
## (Eugenes fulgens)

The magnificent hummingbird is one of the largest hummingbirds in the United States, its body can measure over 5 inches long. The bird has a size similar to the blue-throated hummer, except with a purple head and a darker metallic green color over its entire body.

These birds like to nest high in their environment, most often near the tops of oak, sycamore or pine trees in low mountain slopes. Magnificent hummers are found in western New Mexico and southeastern Arizona from April until November; they travel south into central Mexico during the winter months.

Because they locate in isolated areas and perch high within their feeding territories, they are mildly territorial and do not have to fight other birds for territorial dominance.

Photo © Richard Day/Daybreak Imagery, magnificent male hummingbird

Photo © Frank Cleland / Gnass Photo Images, magnificent male hummingbird

Photo © Steve Aulston, magnificent female hummingbird

page nineteen

# Broad-billed Hummingbirds
## (Cynanthus latirostris)

Broad-billed hummingbirds are larger than average hummingbirds, measuring about 4 inches long, and are less nimble than other species of hummers. They compensate for this by making a continual "chatter" noise during flight that drives competitors away from their nesting and feeding sites.

These birds don't roam very far into the United States, instead they remain in Mexico and venture into southern Arizona, California, western Texas and far southwestern New Mexico during the migrating season. In the winter, they can be commonly found in Guadalajara, Mexico feeding on blossoming wildflowers.

Photo © Hugh P. Smith, broad-billed hummingbird

page twenty

Photo © Frank Cleland/Gnass Photo Images, broad-billed female hummingbird

Photo © Hugh P. Smith, broad-billed hummingbird, feeding fledgling

# Broad-billed Hummingbirds *(Cynanthus latirostris)*

page twenty-two

# Lucifer Hummingbirds
## (Calothorax lucifer)

The lucifer hummingbird is one of the smallest species in North America, with the females being significantly larger than the males. Males have metallic violet gorgets with spotted coloring along their sides and bellies, while females have white patches under their chins and white tips on their tail feathers.

They migrate into the southwestern United States only, breeding in western Texas, southern New Mexico and southeastern Arizona. Tending to reside on desert plateaus and mountain slopes, they build their nests in cacti or shrubs. The flowering agave is the most attractive flower to these hummingbirds because it attracts insects and produces a large quantity of tasty nectar.

The name "lucifer" refers to its scientific name Calothorax lucifer that translates from the Greek to "beautiful chest light bearer."

Photo © Steve Aulston, lucifer male hummingbird

Photo © Steve Aulston, lucifer male hummingbird

# Blue-throated Hummingbirds
## (Lampornis clemenciae)

Although it is considered to be a Mexican species, the blue-throated hummer does spend its summer in parts of Arizona, southwest New Mexico and western Texas. It is a large bird, often measuring up to 5¼ inches long. Males have metallic blue chins and throats, with their backs and chests a deep dull green. The females have similar coloring as the males, except without the blue patches on their chins and with white flecks on their tail feathers.

These hummers prefer to nest in wooded areas near streams and dense vegetation. Their nests are often in high covered areas, appearing bulky and large compared to other hummingbirds. Favorite feeding flowers include agave, sage and cardinal flowers, but the blue-throated species does rely on a heavy diet of insects and spiders.

This is a very aggressive species; its call is a loud high-pitched squeak that it gives in flight or while feeding as a warning to others. It competes with magnificent, violet-crowned and black-chinned hummingbirds for food and breeding territory every summer.

Photo © Steve Aulston, blue-throated male hummingbird

Photo © Steve Aulston, blue-throated male hummingbird

Photo © Steve Aulston, blue-throated male hummingbird

page twenty-five

# Costa's Hummingbirds
## (Calypte costae)

Of all of the hummingbirds who nest in the western part of the United States, Costa's is the one that prefers the driest environment. They tend to settle into desert and arid regions that are located far from water sources, building nests in trees, shrubs and cacti. Costa's hummingbird set up year-round colonies in southern Nevada, western Arizona, southern California and occasionally in Texas, Utah and Oregon. Like all other hummers, they feed off of nectar producing flowers, but as the desert sun dries this foliage out, they migrate west.

Although they are territorial, their main competition is their own species. Males separate their perching areas from female nesting areas and often fight females for territorial control. Their call is a sharp high-pitched "chirp" that sounds like a ricocheting bullet, when the males dive to attract females during courtship, they emit a soft musical whistle at the end of the dive.

Mature male Costa's hummingbirds are medium-sized, about 3-3½ inches long, with metallic purple chins and throats. Females are about the same size as the males, but with darker colored heads and without the coloring on their chins and throats.

Photo © Steve Aulston, Costa's male hummingbird

Photo © Steve Aulston, Costa's male hummingbird

Photo © Hugh P. Smith, Jr., Costa's female hummingbird

page twenty-seven

# Anna's Hummingbirds
## (Calypte anna)

A unique bird because the male Anna's hummingbird is the only North American hummingbird with a fully red head. Both males and females have green backs and wings and are generally the same size, measuring about 3½-4 inches in length.

Anna's hummer is a permanent resident of California, southern Nevada, most of Arizona, western Texas and southern New Mexico. Nests are built in vines, shrubs and trees in forests, chaparral, canyons and mountain slopes.

They inhabit the same areas as Allen's and rufous hummingbirds and are quite territorial, with the females being just as aggressive as the males when it comes to defending feeding sites.

The hummingbird gets its name from Anna de Belle Massena, the Duchess of Rivoli, wife of nineteenth century French bird enthusiast and natural historian Duc de Rivoli, for whom the magnificent hummingbird is given its common name, Rivoli's hummingbird.

Photo © Steve Aulston, Anna's male hummingbird

Photo © Hugh P. Smith, Jr., Anna's male hummingbird

Photo © Steve Aulston, Anna's male hummingbird

page twenty-nine

# Anna's Hummingbirds (Calypte anna)

Photo © Hugh P. Smith, Jr., Anna's male hummingbird

Photo © Steve Aulston, Anna's male hummingbird

# Black-chinned Hummingbirds
### (Archilochus alexandri)

The black-chinned hummingbird is medium sized with a metallic green back and head. Males have metallic-purple coloring on their throats and chins and white tufts on their bellies. Females have less coloring than the males and tend to have darker heads and grayish-white bellies.

Found across the western part of the United States with occasional sightings in the gulf states east to Florida, black-chinned hummers nest in cultivated fields, irrigated areas, orchards and even in mountainous regions. They typically nest between 3-10 feet above ground level, feeding off of small insects and blooming mountain flowers. Both males and females chase flying insects, but the males tend to vacate nesting areas soon after settling them, leaving available food for females and young hummers.

Photo © Steve Aulston, black-chinned male hummingbird

Photo © Steve Aulston, black-chinned male hummingbird

# Black-chinned Hummingbirds (Archilochus alexandri)

Photo © Hugh P. Smith, Jr., black-chinned hummingbird

Photo © Hugh P. Smith, Jr., black-chinned female hummingbird

Photo © Hugh P. Smith, Jr., black-chinned hummingbirds, 20 days old

page thirty-two